All-Americans

by Elaine Roche-Tombee
illustrated by John Dollar

Chapters

Harcourt

Orlando   Boston   Dallas   Chicago   San Diego

Visit *The Learning Site!*

www.harcourtschool.com

No More Baseball?

In 1943 the United States was at war. Millions of Americans were in the armed forces. Women at home were needed to work at jobs that had always been held by men. This is the story of some of those women.

Few men were immune to being drafted into the army. Baseball players were no exception. At the war's peak, more than 300 major-league players were serving their country. Some minor leagues had to stop playing. They did not have enough players.

Americans wanted to keep going to baseball games. Baseball was something that consoled them during these hard times. Club owners worked hard to put together teams. A fifteen-year-old boy pitched for the Cincinnati Reds. A one-armed outfielder played one amazing season for the St. Louis Browns.

Philip K. Wrigley was the owner of the Chicago Cubs. He had a different idea for keeping baseball going. He started a new league—for women.

There had been women's baseball clubs as early as 1867. Lizzie Arlington had pitched in a minor-league game in 1898. Several women had played in preseason games with major-league teams. One of them was a seventeen-year-old pitcher named Jackie Mitchell.

Jackie Mitchell played for the Chattanooga Lookouts. They were a minor-league team in Tennessee. In April 1931, the New York Yankees stopped in Chattanooga for a game. Nearly 4,000 people came to watch this famous team play the Lookouts.

Another pitcher started the game for the Lookouts. However, he gave up too many runs. The Lookouts' manager told Jackie to take his place.

The first Yankee batter that Jackie faced was Babe Ruth. She struck him out! The next batter was Lou Gehrig. Jackie struck him out, too!

The crowd stood and cheered the young pitcher. Soon, though, the Lookouts' manager had to replace her with another pitcher. In the end, the Yankees beat the Lookouts, 14-4.

About 40,000 women were playing in softball leagues in 1943. Wrigley guessed he would have no trouble finding 60 players. That spring he held tryouts in Chicago. The most favored best players received invitations. Hundreds simply showed up.

The "Girls" League

Four teams trotted out onto the ball fields that first season. They were from Rockford, Illinois; South Bend, Indiana; and Kenosha and Racine, Wisconsin. Together they formed the All-American Girls' Professional Baseball League.

The players were called "girls" even though most of them were over eighteen. They came from all over the United States and from Canada and Cuba as well.

By 1946, eight teams were playing 110 games a summer. They played a game every day of the week and a double-header on Sundays. As soon as a game was over, the teams boarded buses for the next city. Often they arrived just in time to play another game. They even had to sleep on the bus.

For all this, the "girls" were paid from $50 to $125 a week. Most players were factory workers and farm women. To them, this was good pay. Some would even have played for nothing.

However, the players did not like their uniforms. League rules made them play in skirts. Their first uniforms had long skirts that got in the way of fielding and pitching. The skirts were soon shortened to well above the knees so the players could play.

However, the shorter skirts created another problem. Even when wearing long pants, players can get hurt as they slide into base. Most of the women had scraped and bruised legs from sliding in their short skirts.

Not only that, but strong winds often caught the players' skirts. How could they play baseball while holding down their skirts? Years later, however, many former players still have their uniforms. They keep them as reminders of the fun they had playing for their teams.

There were other rules. The women were sup-
posed to be well behaved, on and off the field. A
player might glare at an umpire, but she could be
fined for arguing. Nevertheless, many players did
more than glare. The All-Americans could be as
tough and competitive as the male players.

Charm School for the Players

Wrigley was determined to have his players look and behave like ladies. He even set up a "charm school" for them. They had to study a ten-page booklet called "A Guide for All-American Girls: How to Look Better, Feel Better, and Be More Popular."

The players were taught to sit, walk, and stand "like young ladies." They learned how to care for their faces and their hair. They were expected to wear make-up on the field. The players also had to keep their hair long.

Wrigley wanted attractive, polite, ladylike athletes on his teams. He hired chaperones to go with them on their rare shopping or sightseeing trips. He told them how late they could stay out at night. Most of the women put up with all of these rules, because they wanted to play baseball.

More than 175,000 fans turned out that first season. Fans in all the league's cities turned out to support their teams. The Racine Belles were favored to win the pennant, and they did.

More teams were added for the 1944 season. Attendance went up by more than half. In 1945 attendance doubled. The league was an amazing success.

The league's big test came the following year. The war was over, and the men's major and minor leagues were back at full strength. Still the All-American Girls' Professional Baseball League continued to be successful. At its peak in 1948, the league drew one million fans. Women's professional baseball seemed to be here to stay.

Stars Shine

Some of the players became stars. Jean Faut of the South Bend Blue Sox was the league's best pitcher. She had 132 wins and lost only 62 games. Twice she pitched "perfect games."

Dorothy Kamenshek was a top hitter. In fact, she struck out only 81 times out of 3,736 times at bat. She played first base for the Rockford Peaches. A former New York Yankees player called Kamenshek "the fanciest-fielding first base-man I've ever seen—man or woman."

Alma "Gabby" Ziegler played second base for the Grand Rapids Chicks. Her playing and personality made her a team leader for eleven years.

Shortstop Dorothy Schroeder was only fifteen when she joined the Blue Sox. She played in the league for all of its twelve seasons. Charlie Grimm, the Chicago Cubs manager, said of her, "If she were a boy, I'd give $50,000 for her."

Sophie Kurys played for the Racine Belles. She was the league's fastest runner. In 1946, Kurys stole 201 bases. The most bases stolen by any male player in the major leagues is 130, many fewer than Kurys. And remember that Kurys stole all those bases while wearing a short skirt!

Losing the League?

After 1948 the All-American Girls' Professional Baseball League started to lose fans. There were many reasons for this. The league shifted players from team to team. Rules and equipment were often changed in the middle of the season. There was no system for developing new players. The league had never caught on in the big cities.

Another reason for the loss of fans was the growth of television. People in the leagues' cities could now watch major-league baseball without leaving home.

The All-American league played its last season in 1954. Although it did not survive very long, the women involved had truly been professional baseball players.

Some of the women began to play on softball teams. Most found jobs outside of sports. Some used the money they had earned as players to go to college.

Many of the players married and had families. One was Helen St. Aubin. She had led the league in batting in 1945. Her son, Casey Candaele, later played in the major leagues.

In 1988 the National Baseball Hall of Fame
opened an exhibit called "Women in Baseball."
Many of the league's former players donated
mementoes. The exhibit quickly became one of the
museum's most popular attractions.

The women who played in the league hold fre-
quent reunions. They are often asked by reporters
to talk about their playing days. Most of them give
the same answer: "They were the best years of
my life."